Born in 1962

by

Kerry Butters.

Born in 1962

Millennium:	**2nd millennium**
Centuries:	19th century – **20th century** – 21st century
Decades:	1930s 1940s 1950s – **1960s** – 1970s 1980s 1990s
Years:	1959 1960 1961 – **1962** – 1963 1964 1965

1962 (MCMLXII) was a common year starting on Monday (dominical letter G) of the Gregorian calendar, the 1962nd year of the Common Era (CE) and *Anno Domini* (AD) designations, the 962nd year of the 2nd millennium, the 62nd year of the 20th century, and the 3rd year of the 1960s decade.

Contents

Events

January

- January 1
  - Western Samoa becomes independent from New Zealand.
  - The United States Navy SEALs, elite special forces, are activated. SEAL Team One is commissioned in the Pacific Fleet and SEAL Team Two in the Atlantic Fleet.
  - The Beatles audition for Decca Records but are rejected.
  - NBC introduces the "Laramie peacock" before a midnight showing of the series *Laramie* in the United States.
- January 2 – NAACP Executive Secretary Roy Wilkins praises U.S. President John F. Kennedy's "personal role" in advancing civil rights.
- January 3 – Pope John XXIII excommunicates Fidel Castro.
- January 4 – New York City introduces a subway train that operates without a crew on board.
- January 5 – The first album on which The Beatles play, *My Bonnie*, credited to "Tony Sheridan and the Beat Brothers" (recorded last June in Hamburg), is released by Polydor in the U.K.
- January 8 – Harmelen train disaster: 93 die in the worst Dutch rail disaster.
- January 9 – Cuba and the Soviet Union sign a trade pact.
- January 10 – An avalanche on Nevado Huascarán in Peru causes 4,000 deaths.
- January 12 – The Indonesian Army confirms that it has begun operations in West Irian.

- January 13 – Albania allies itself with the People's Republic of China.
- January 15 – Portugal abandons the U.N. General Assembly due to the debate over Angola.
- January 16 – A military coup occurs in the Dominican Republic.
- January 19 – A counter-coup occurs in the Dominican Republic; the old government returns except for the new president Rafael Filiberto Bonnelly.
- January 22 – The Organization of American States suspends Cuba's membership. The suspension is lifted in 2009.
- January 24
  - The East German government readopts conscription.
  - The Organisation de l'armée secrète (OAS) bombs the French Foreign Ministry.
- January 26 – Ranger 3 is launched to study the Moon; it later misses the Moon by 22,000 miles.
- January 27 – The Soviet government changed all place names honoring Molotov, Kaganovich and Georgy Malenkov.
- January 30 – Two of the high-wire "Flying Wallendas" are killed, when their famous seven-person pyramid collapses during a performance in Detroit.
- January – Stena Line is established as a ferry operator by Sten A. Olsson in Gothenburg, Sweden.

February

- February 3 – The United States embargo against Cuba is announced.
- February 4 – *The Sunday Times* in the United Kingdom became the first paper to print a colour supplement.
- February 4–February 5 – During a new moon and solar eclipse, an extremely rare grand conjunction of the classical planets occurs (it includes all five of the naked-eye planets plus the Sun and Moon), all of them within 16° of one another on the ecliptic.
- February 5 – French President Charles de Gaulle calls for Algeria to be granted independence.

- February 6 – Negotiations between U.S. Steel and the United States Department of Commerce begin.
- February 7
  - The United States embargo against Cuba comes into effect, prohibiting all U.S.-related Cuban imports and exports.
  - Luisenthal Mine Disaster: A coal mine explosion in Saarland, West Germany kills 299.
- February 9 – The Taiwan Stock Exchange Corporation opens.
- February 10 – Captured American spy pilot Francis Gary Powers is exchanged for captured Soviet spy Rudolf Abel in Berlin.
- February 11 – The inaugural 24 Hours of Daytona sports car endurance race is run as a 3-hour event at Daytona Beach, Florida.
- February 12 – Six members of the Committee of 100 of the Campaign for Nuclear Disarmament in the U.K. are found guilty of a breach of the Official Secrets Act.
- February 14 – First Lady Jacqueline Kennedy takes television viewers on a tour of the White House.
- February 15 – Urho Kekkonen is re-elected president of Finland.
- February 16 – Heavy storms flood Germany's North Sea coast, mainly around Hamburg; more than 300 people die and thousands lose their homes.
- February 20 – Project Mercury: While aboard *Friendship 7*, John Glenn became the first American to orbit the Earth, three times in 4 hours, 55 minutes.
- February 21 – Margot Fonteyn and Rudolf Nureyev first dance together in a Royal Ballet performance of *Giselle* in London.

February 23: *Friendship 7* inspected by President Kennedy and Astronaut John Glenn

March

- March 1
  - American Airlines Flight 1 (a Boeing 707) crashes on takeoff at New York International Airport, after a rudder malfunction causes an uncontrolled roll, resulting in the loss of control of the aircraft, with the loss of all 95 on board.
  - The S. S. Kresge Company opens its first Kmart discount store in Garden City, Michigan.
- March 2
  - A military coup in Burma brings General Ne Win to power.
  - Wilt Chamberlain's 100-point game: Wilt Chamberlain scored 100 points in a single National Basketball Association basketball game.
- March 7 – Ash Wednesday Storm: A snow storm batters the Mid-Atlantic.
- March 8–12 – In Geneva, France and the Algerian FLN begin negotiations.
- March 15 – Katangan Prime Minister Moise Tshombe begins negotiations to rejoin the Congo.
- March 16 – Flying Tiger Line Flight 739, a Lockheed L-1049H Super Constellation chartered by the United States Military Air Transport Service and carrying mainly United States Army personnel bound for South Vietnam, vanishes over the western Pacific Ocean with the loss of all 107 on board. No wreckage or bodies are ever found.
- March 18
  - Évian Accords: France and Algeria sign an agreement in Évian-les-Bains ending the Algerian War.
  - *Un premier amour*, sung by Isabelle Aubret (music by Claude-Henri Vic, lyrics by Roland Stephane Valade), wins the Eurovision Song Contest 1962 for France.
- March 19
  - An armistice begins in Algeria; however, the OAS continues its terrorist attacks against Algerians.
  - Bob Dylan's debut album is released in the United States.

- March 21 – Taco Bell fast food restaurant chain is founded by Glen Bell in Downey, California.
- March 23 – The Scandinavian States of the Nordic Council sign the Helsinki Convention on Nordic Co-operation.
- March 24 – OAS leader Edmond Jouhaud is arrested in Oran.
- March 26
  - France shortens the term for military service from 26 months to 18.
  - *Baker v. Carr*: The U.S. Supreme Court rules that federal courts can order state legislatures to reapportion seats.

April

- April 3 – Jawaharlal Nehru is elected de facto Prime Minister of India.
- April 4 – James Hanratty is hanged in Bedford Gaol (England) for the A6 murder; many believe he was innocent.
- April 6
  - Belgium reestablishes diplomatic relations with the Congo.
  - New York Philharmonic concert of April 6, 1962: Leonard Bernstein causes controversy with his remarks before a concert featuring Glenn Gould with the New York Philharmonic, when he (Bernstein) announces that although he disagrees with Gould's style of playing Brahms' Piano Concerto No. 1, he finds Gould's ideas fascinating and will conduct the piece anyway. Bernstein's action receives a withering review from *The New York Times* music critic Harold C. Schonberg.
- April 7 – Milovan Đilas, author and former vice-president of Yugoslavia is re-arrested.
- April 8 – In France, the Évian Accords are adopted in a referendum with a majority of 90%.
- April 9 – The 34th Academy Awards ceremony is held; *West Side Story* wins Best Picture.
- April 10 – In Los Angeles, the first MLB baseball game is played at Dodger Stadium.

- April 13 – OAS leader Edmond Jouhaud is sentenced to death in France.
- April 14 – A Cuban military tribunal convicts 1,179 Bay of Pigs attackers.
- April 18 – The Commonwealth Immigration Bill in the United Kingdom removes free immigration from the citizens of member states of the Commonwealth of Nations.
- April 20 – OAS leader Raoul Salan is arrested in Algiers.
- April 21 – The Century 21 Exposition World's Fair opens in Seattle.
- April 26 – The Ranger 4 spacecraft crashes into the Moon.

May

- May – Larry Allen Abshier defects to North Korea becoming the first of six (possibly seven) American defectors to the country.
- May 1
  - Norwich City F.C. wins the English Football League Cup, beating Rochdale in the final.
  - Dayton Hudson Corporation opens the first of its Target discount stores in Roseville, Minnesota.
- May 2
  - An OAS bomb explodes in Algeria – this and other attacks kill 110 and injure 147.
  - S.L. Benfica beats FC Barcelona 5-3 at the Olympic Stadium (Amsterdam) to win the 1961–62 European Cup in association football.
- May 3 – Mikawashima train crash: 160 die in a triple-train disaster near Tokyo.
- May 5 – Twelve East Germans escape via a tunnel under the Berlin Wall.
- May 6 – Antonio Segni is elected President of the Italian Republic.
- May 14
  - Juan Carlos of Spain marries the Greek Princess Sophia in Athens.

- o Milovan Đilas is given a further sentence in Yugoslavia for publishing *Conversations with Stalin*.
- May 22 – Continental Airlines Flight 11 crashes near Unionville, Missouri, after the in-flight detonation of a bomb near the rear lavatory. All 45 passengers and crew aboard are killed.
- May 23
  - o Drilling for the new Montreal subway commences.
  - o Raoul Salan, founder of the French terrorist Organisation armée secrète, is sentenced to life imprisonment in France.
- May 24 – Project Mercury: Scott Carpenter orbits the Earth 3 times in the *Aurora 7* space capsule.
- May 25 – The new Coventry Cathedral is consecrated in England.
- May 26 – Acker Bilk's *Stranger on the Shore* becomes the first British recording to reach number one in the US Billboard Hot 100.
- May 27 – The Centralia mine fire is ignited in Pennsylvania.
- May 29 – Negotiations between the OAS and the FLA lead to a real armistice in Algeria.
- May 30 – The beginning of the 1962 FIFA World Cup in Chile.
- May 31 – Nazi Adolf Eichmann is hanged at a prison in Ramla, Israel. His body is cremated and his ashes scattered over the Mediterranean.

June

- June 3 – Air France Flight 007 (a Boeing 707) crashes on take-off at Orly Airport in Paris; 130 of 132 people on board are killed, 2 flight attendants survive. Most victims are cultural and civic leaders of Atlanta.
- June 6 – President John F. Kennedy gives the commencement address at the United States Military Academy at West Point, New York.
- June 11
  - o President John F. Kennedy gives the commencement address at Yale University.

- o Frank Morris, John Anglin and Clarence Anglin escape from the Alcatraz Island prison; the men are never heard from again.
- June 15 – Students for a Democratic Society in the United States complete the Port Huron Statement.
- June 17
  - o The OAS signs a truce with the FLN in Algeria, but a day later announces that it will continue the fight on behalf of French Algerians.
  - o Brazil beats Czechoslovakia 3–1 to win the 1962 FIFA World Cup.
- June 22 – Air France Flight 117 (a Boeing 707 jet) crashes into terrain during bad weather in Guadeloupe, West Indies, killing all 113 on board, the airline's second fatal accident in just 3 weeks, and the third fatal 707 crash of the year.
- June 25
  - o *Engel v. Vitale*: The United States Supreme Court rules that mandatory prayers in public schools are unconstitutional.
  - o *MANual Enterprises v. Day*: The United States Supreme Court rules that photographs of nude men are not obscene, decriminalizing nude male pornographic magazines.
  - o İsmet İnönü of CHP forms the new government of Turkey (27th government, coalition partners; YTP and CKMP)
- June 26 – A 2-day steel strike begins in Italy in support of increased wages and a five-day working week.
- June 28 – The United Lutheran Church in America, Finnish Evangelical Lutheran Church of America, American Evangelical Lutheran Church and Augustana Evangelical Lutheran Church merge to form the Lutheran Church in America.
- June 30 – The last soldiers of the French Foreign Legion leave Algeria.
- June – Rachel Carson's *Silent Spring* begins serialization in *The New Yorker*; it is released as a book on September 27 in the U.S., giving rise to the modern environmentalist movement.
-

July

- July 1
  - Rwanda and Burundi gain independence.
  - Algerian independence referendum, 1962: Supporters of Algerian independence win 99% majority in a referendum.
  - A heavy smog develops over London.
  - Helsinki Convention on Nordic Co-operation of March 23 comes into force in the Nordic countries.
- July 2
  - Charles de Gaulle accepts Algerian independence; France recognizes it the next day.
  - The first Walmart store, at this time known as *Wal-Mart* (which remains the corporate name), opens for business in Rogers, Arkansas.
- July 5 – Algeria becomes independent from France.
- July 6 – Gay Byrne presents the first edition of *The Late Late Show* on RTÉ in the Republic of Ireland. Byrne goes on to present the show for 37 years, the longest period through which any individual hosts a televised talk show anywhere in the world, and the show itself becomes the world's second longest-running talk show.
- July 9 – American artist Andy Warhol premieres his *Campbell's Soup Cans* exhibit in Los Angeles.
- July 10 – AT&T's Telstar, the world's first commercial communications satellite, is launched into orbit and activated the next day.
- July 12 – The Rolling Stones make their debut at London's Marquee Club, Number 165 Oxford Street, opening for Long John Baldry.
- July 13 – In what the press dubs "the Night of the Long Knives", United Kingdom Prime Minister Harold Macmillan dismisses one-third of his Cabinet.
- July 17 – Nuclear testing: The "Small Boy" test shot Little Feller I became the last atmospheric test detonation at the Nevada Test Site.

- July 19 – The first annual Swiss & Wielder Hoop and Stick Tournament is held.
- July 20 – France and Tunisia reestablish diplomatic relations.
- July 22 – Mariner program: The Mariner 1 spacecraft flies erratically several minutes after launch and has to be destroyed.
- July 23 – Telstar relays the first live trans-Atlantic television signal.
- July 25
  - The first armed helicopter company of the United States Army is formed at Okinawa, Japan.
  - The International Agreement on the Neutrality of Laos is signed in Geneva.
- July 31
  - Algeria proclaims independence; Ahmed Ben Bella is the first President.
  - A crowd assaults the rally of Sir Oswald Mosley's right-wing Union Movement in London.

August

- August 5
  - Death of Marilyn Monroe: Marilyn Monroe is found dead from an overdose of sleeping pills and chloral hydrate at her home in Brentwood, Los Angeles; officially ruled a "probable suicide" (the exact cause has been disputed).
  - Nelson Mandela is arrested by the South African government near Howick and charged with incitement to rebellion
- August 6 – Jamaica becomes independent.
- August 15 – The New York Agreement is signed, trading the West New Guinea colony to Indonesia.
- August 16
  - Beatles drummer Pete Best is dismissed and replaced by Ringo Starr.
  - Algeria joins the Arab League.
- August 17 – East German border guards kill 18-year-old Peter Fechter as he attempts to cross the Berlin Wall into West Berlin

- August 22 – A failed assassination attempt is made against French President Charles de Gaulle.
- August 23 – John Lennon marries Cynthia Powell in an unpublicised register office ceremony at Mount Pleasant, Liverpool.
- August 24 – A group of armed Cuban exile terrorists fire at a hotel in Havana from a speedboat.
- August 27 – NASA launches the *Mariner 2* space probe.
- August 31 – Trinidad and Tobago becomes independent.

September

- September 1
  - A referendum in Singapore supports the Malayan Federation.
  - Typhoon Wanda strikes Hong Kong, killing at least 130 and injuring more than 600.
- September 2 – The Soviet Union agrees to send arms to Cuba.
- September 8 – Newly independent Algeria, by referendum, adopts a constitution.
- September 12 – President John F. Kennedy, at a speech at Rice University, reaffirms that the U.S. will put a man on the moon by the end of the decade.
- September 19 – Atlantic College opens its doors for the first time in Wales, marking the birth of the pioneering United World College educational movement.
- September 21 – A border conflict between China and India erupts into fighting.
- September 22 – 21-year-old Bob Dylan premieres one of his most preeminent songs, "A Hard Rain's a-Gonna Fall", in the U.S.
- September 23 – The animated sitcom *The Jetsons* premieres on ABC in the U.S.
- September 25 – Sonny Liston knocks out Floyd Patterson two minutes into the first round of his fight for the boxing world title in Chicago.
- September 26 – North Yemen Civil War erupts.

- September 27 – A flash flood in Barcelona, Spain, kills more than 440 people.
- September 29 – The Canadian *Alouette 1*, the first satellite built outside the United States and the Soviet Union, is launched from Vandenberg Air Force Base in California.
- September 30 – CBS broadcasts the final episodes of *Suspense* and *Yours Truly, Johnny Dollar*, marking the end of the Golden Age of Radio in the United States.

October

October 14: Pictures of Soviet missile silos in Cuba, taken by US spy planes

- October 1
  - The first black student, James Meredith, registers at the University of Mississippi, escorted by Federal Marshals.
  - Johnny Carson takes over as permanent host of NBC's *The Tonight Show* in the U.S., a post he will hold for 30 years.
  - Lucille Ball and Vivian Vance return to television with *The Lucy Show*, two years after the end of *I Love Lucy*. Vance becomes the first person to portray a divorcée on a weekly series.
- October 3 – Project Mercury: Mercury-Atlas 8 – Walter Schirra orbits the Earth six times in the *Sigma 7* space capsule.
- October 5
  - The French National Assembly censures the proposed referendum to sanction presidential elections by popular

mandate; Prime Minister Georges Pompidou resigns, but President de Gaulle asks him to stay in office.
- The Beatles' first single in their own right, "Love Me Do"/"P.S. I Love You", is released in the U.K. on EMI's Parlophone label. This version was recorded on September 4 at Abbey Road Studios in London with Ringo Starr as drummer.
- *Dr. No*, the first James Bond film, premieres at the London Pavilion, featuring Sean Connery as the hero.
- October 8
  - The German magazine *Der Spiegel* publishes an article about the Bundeswehr's poor preparedness; the *Spiegel* scandal erupts.
  - Algeria is accepted into the United Nations.
- October 9 – Uganda becomes independent within the Commonwealth of Nations.
- October 10 – The beginning of Sino-Indian War, a border dispute involving two of the world's largest nations (India and the People's Republic of China).
- October 11 – Second Vatican Council: Pope John XXIII convenes the first ecumenical council of the Roman Catholic Church in 92 years.
- October 12
  - The infamous Columbus Day Storm strikes the U.S. Pacific Northwest with wind gusts up to 170 mph (270 km/h); 46 are killed, 11 billion board feet (26 million m³) of timber is blown down, with $230 million U.S. in damages.
  - Jazz bassist/composer Charles Mingus invites the public to a live recording session at The Town Hall (New York City), but the public is expecting a formal concert. Along with technical problems the event is the worst moment of his career.
- October 13 – Broadway debut of Edward Albee's drama *Who's Afraid of Virginia Woolf?*.
- October 14 – The beginning of the Cuban Missile Crisis: A U-2 flight over Cuba in the Caribbean photographs Soviet nuclear

weapons being installed. A stand-off then ensues for another 12 days after President Kennedy is told of the pictures, between the United States and the Soviet Union, threatening the world with nuclear war.

- October 19 – Establishment of Thái Nguyên City, under Thái Nguyên, in Vietnam.
- October 22 – Cuban Missile Crisis: In a televised address, U.S. President John F. Kennedy announces to the nation the existence of Soviet missiles in Cuba.
- October 24 – Cuban Missile Crisis: First confrontation between the U.S. Navy and a Soviet cargo vessel. The vessel changes course.
- October 26 – *Spiegel* scandal: German police occupy *Der Spiegel* offices in Hamburg.
- October 28
  - The end of the Cuban Missile Crisis: Soviet Union leader Nikita Khrushchev announces that he has ordered the removal of Soviet missile bases in Cuba. In a secret deal between Kennedy and Khrushchev, Kennedy agrees to the withdrawal of U.S. missiles from Turkey. The fact that this deal was not made public makes it look as though the Soviets have backed down.
  - A referendum in France favors the election of the president by universal suffrage.
- October 31 – The United Nations General Assembly asks the United Kingdom to suspend enforcement of the new constitution in Southern Rhodesia (now Zimbabwe), but it comes into effect on November 1.

November

- November – Aleksandr Solzhenitsyn's novella *One Day in the Life of Ivan Denisovich* (Russian: Один день Ивана Денисовича, *Odin den' Ivana Denisovicha*), the author's semi-autobiographical account of life in the gulag, is published in *Novy Mir* in an unprecedented acknowledgement of the Soviet Union's Stalinist past.

- November 1
  - The Soviets begin dismantling their missiles in Cuba.
  - First appearance of comic book antihero Diabolik in Italy.
- November 3 – Earliest recorded use of the term "personal computer" in the report of a speech by computing pioneer John Mauchly in *The New York Times*.
- November 5
  - Franz Josef Strauß, the West German defense minister, is relieved of his duties over the *Spiegel* scandal, due to his alleged involvement in police action against the magazine.
  - Saudi Arabia breaks off diplomatic relations with Egypt, following a period of unrest partly caused by the defection of several Saudi princes to Egypt.
  - A coal mining disaster in Ny-Ålesund killed 21 people. The Norwegian government is forced to resign in the aftermath of this accident in August 1963.
- November 6 – Apartheid: The United Nations General Assembly passes a resolution condemning South Africa's racist apartheid policies and calls for all UN member states to cease military and economic relations with the nation.
- November 7 – Richard M. Nixon loses the California governor's race. In his concession speech, he states that this is "Richard Nixon's last press conference" and "you won't have Nixon to kick around any more".
- November 17 – Dulles International Airport in Washington, D.C., dedicated by President John F. Kennedy.
- November 20 – Cuban missile crisis: In response to the Soviet Union agreeing to remove its missiles from Cuba, President John F. Kennedy ends the blockade of the island.
- November 21 – The Sino-Indian War ends with a Chinese ceasefire.
- November 23 – United Airlines Flight 297 crashes in Columbia, Maryland, killing all 17 on board.
- November 24 – The first episode of the groundbreaking satirical comedy program *That Was the Week That Was*, hosted by David Frost is broadcast on BBC Television in the U.K.

- November 26
  - *Spiegel* scandal: German police end their occupation of *Der Spiegel*'s offices.
  - Mies Bouwman starts presenting the first live TV-marathon fundraising show (*Open Het Dorp* in the Netherlands), which lasts 23 hours non-stop.
- November 27 – French President Charles De Gaulle orders Georges Pompidou to form a government.
- November 29 – An agreement is signed between Britain and France to develop the *Concorde* supersonic airliner.
- November 30 – The United Nations General Assembly elects U Thant of Burma as the new Secretary-General of the United Nations.

December

- December 2 – Vietnam War: After a trip to Vietnam at the request of U.S. President John F. Kennedy, U.S. Senate Majority Leader Mike Mansfield becomes the first American official to make a non-optimistic public comment on the war's progress.
- December 7 – Rainier III, Prince of Monaco revises the principality's constitution, devolving some of his formerly autocratic power to several advisory and legislative councils.
- December 8
  - The first period of the Second Vatican Council closes.
  - The North Kalimantan National Army revolts in Brunei, in the first stirrings of the Indonesian Confrontation.
  - The 1962–63 New York City newspaper strike begins, affecting all of the city's major newspapers; It will last for 114 days.
  - Queen Wilhelmina of the Netherlands, who died on November 28, is buried at the Nieuwe Kerk (Delft).
- December 9 – Tanganyika (modern-day Tanzania) becomes a republic within the Commonwealth of Nations, with Julius Nyerere as president.

- December 10 – David Lean's epic film *Lawrence of Arabia*, featuring Peter O'Toole, Omar Sharif, Alec Guinness, Jack Hawkins and Anthony Quinn, premieres in London. Six days later it opens in the U.S.
- December 11
  - In West Germany, a coalition government of Christian Democrats, Christian Socialists and Free Democrats is formed.
  - The last execution by hanging in Canada
- December 14
  - U.S. spacecraft Mariner 2 passes by Venus, becoming the first probe to transmit data successfully from another planet.
  - Leonardo da Vinci's early 16th-century painting the *Mona Lisa* is assessed for insurance purposed at US$100 million before touring the United States for several months, the highest insurance value for a painting in history. However, the Louvre, its owner, chooses to spend the money that would have been spent on the insurance premium on security instead.
- December 15 – Storm over the North Sea: Belgian pirate radio station Radio Uylenspiegel is knocked off the airwaves, never to operate again.
- December 19 – Britain acknowledged the right of Nyasaland (modern-day Malawi) to secede from the Central African Federation.
- December 21 – Britain agrees to purchase Polaris missiles from the U.S.
- December 22 – Winter of 1962–63 in the United Kingdom: The "Big Freeze" begins; there are no frost-free nights until March 5, 1963.
- December 24 – Cuba releases the last 1,113 participants in the Bay of Pigs Invasion to the U.S., in exchange for food worth $53 million.
- December 30
  - United Nations troops occupy the last rebel positions in Katanga; Moise Tshombe moves to South Rhodesia.

o An unexpected storm buries Maine under five feet of snow, forcing the *Bangor Daily News* to miss a publication date for the only time in history. The same day, also the Netherlands were covered with several feet of snow.

Date unknown

- American advertising man Martin K. Speckter invents the interrobang, a new English-language punctuation mark.
- Publication of Helen Gurley Brown's *Sex and the Single Girl* in the U.S.
- Irish folk band The Dubliners is formed at O'Donoghue's Pub in Dublin.
- Invention of the Laser Diode.
- Slavery in Yemen is abolished.

Births

January

Jim Carrey

Abdullah II of Jordan

- January 3 – Guy Pratt, English musician and songwriter
- January 4 – Natalya Bochina, Russian athlete
- January 5 – Suzy Amis, American actress and model
- January 10 – Samira Said, Moroccan singer
- January 11 – Kim Coles, American actress and comedian
- January 13
    - Trace Adkins, American country music singer
    - Kevin Mitchell, American baseball player
- January 14 – Michael McCaul, American politician
- January 17 – Jim Carrey, Canadian actor and comedian
- January 18 – Mike Lynch, American cartoonist
- January 20
    - IKKO, Japanese make-up artist
    - Sakiko Tamagawa, Japanese voice actress

- o Sophie Thompson, English actress
- January 21
  - o Tyler Cowen, American economist
  - o Marie Trintignant, French actress (d. 2003)
- January 22
  - o Mizan Zainal Abidin, current Yang di-Pertuan Agong of Malaysia
  - o Lyudmila Dzhigalova, Russian athlete
- January 23
  - o Stephen Keshi, Nigerian footballer and manager
  - o Richard Roxburgh, Australian actor
- January 25 – Chris Chelios, American ice hockey player
- January 26 – Anna LaCazio, American singer (Cock Robin)
- January 28
  - o Creflo Dollar, American evangelist
  - o Sam Phillips, American singer
- January 30 – King Abdullah II of Jordan

February

Eddie Izzard

Sheryl Crow

Steve Irwin

Adam Baldwin

- February 1 – Takashi Murakami, Japanese pop artist
- February 2 – Andy Fordham, English darts player
- February 3
    - Michele Greene, American actress
- February 4 – Clint Black, American country musician
- February 5 – Jennifer Jason Leigh, American actress
- February 6 – Axl Rose, American rock singer
- February 7
    - Garth Brooks, American country musician
    - David Bryan, American keyboardist (Bon Jovi)
    - Eddie Izzard, British actor and comedian
- February 8 – Malorie Blackman, British-born author
- February 9
    - Lolo Ferrari, French actress (d. 2000)
    - Dany Roland, Brazilian drummer (Metrô), actor, sound designer, film director and record producer
- February 10
    - Cliff Burton, American bassist (Metallica) (d. 1986)
    - Bobby Czyz, American boxer
- February 11 – Sheryl Crow, American singer-songwriter

- February 12
  - Nana Ioseliani, Georgian chess player
  - Jimmy Kirkwood, Irish-born field hockey player
- February 13 – Aníbal Acevedo Vilá, Puerto Rican politician
- February 17 – Lou Diamond Phillips, American actor
- February 18 – Julie Strain, American actress and model
- February 21
  - Vanessa Feltz, British television presenter
  - Chuck Palahniuk, American author
  - David Foster Wallace, American writer (d. 2008)
- February 22
  - Steve Irwin, Australian herpetologist and television personality (d. 2006)
  - Lenda Murray, American bodybuilder
- February 25
- Birgit Fischer, German kayaker
- Junko Ogata, Japanese serial killer
- February 27 – Adam Baldwin, American actor
- February 28 – Angela Bailey, Canadian athlete

March

Jon Bon Jovi

Matthew Broderick

Rosie O'Donnell

Marcia Cross

- March 2
  - Jon Bon Jovi, American singer, songwriter
  - Raimo Summanen, Finnish ice hockey player and coach
- March 3
  - Jackie Joyner-Kersee, American athlete
  - Herschel Walker, American football player

- March 4 – Simon Bisley, British comic book artist
- March 6
  - Andreas Felder, Austrian ski jumper
  - Erika Hess, Swiss alpine skier
- March 7 – Taylor Dayne, American singer
- March 8 – Cecilia Yip, Hong Kong actress
- March 10 – Seiko Matsuda, Japanese pop singer/songwriter
- March 11 – Barbara Alyn Woods, American actress
- March 12 – Darryl Strawberry, American baseball player
- March 16 – Branco Mello, Brazilian singer, actor and writer
- March 18
  - Thomas Ian Griffith, American actor
  - Mike Rowe, American television host
- March 19 – Iván Calderón, Puerto Rican Major League Baseball player (d. 2003)
- March 20 – Stephen Sommers, American film director
- March 21
  - Matthew Broderick, American actor
  - Rosie O'Donnell, American comedian, actress and talk-show host
- March 23
  - Steve Redgrave, English rower
  - Jenny Wright, American actress
- March 24 – Star Jones, American talk show host and publisher
- March 25 – Marcia Cross, American actress
- March 26
  - Eric Allan Kramer, American actor
  - John Stockton, American basketball player
- March 27
  - Jann Arden, Canadian singer
  - John O'Farrell, British author and broadcaster
- March 29 – Ted Failon, Filipino broadcast journalist and radio commentator
- March 30
  - Bil Dwyer, American actor
  - MC Hammer (Stanley Kirk Burrell), American rapper

April

- April 1
  - Samboy Lim, Filipino basketball player
  - Phillip Schofield, British TV presenter
- April 2 – Mark Shulman, American children's author
- April 5 – Kirsan Ilyumzhinov, President of Kalmykia and FIDE
- April 7 – Hugh O'Connor, American actor (d. 1995)
- April 9 – Imran Sherwani, British field hockey player
- April 10
  - Rick Florian, American Christian musician and real estate agent
  - Steve Tasker, American football player
- April 12
  - Carlos Sainz, Spanish rally driver
  - Nobuhiko Takada, Japanese mixed martial arts fighter and professional wrestler
- April 13 – Jennifer Rubin, American actress/model
- April 15
  - Nawal El Moutawakel, Moroccan hurdler
  - Nick Kamen, English singer, songwriter, musician and model
- April 19 – Al Unser, Jr., American race car driver
- April 20 – Hank the Angry Drunken Dwarf (Henry Joseph Nasiff Jr.), American comedian (d. 2001)
- April 23 – John Hannah, Scottish actor
- April 24 – Steve Roach, Australian champion rugby league prop forward
- April 26
  - Colin Anderson, English footballer
  - Michael Damian, American singer and actor

May

Emilio Estevez

François-Henri Pinault

- May 2
  - Elizabeth Berridge, American actress
  - Jimmy White, British snooker player
- May 3 – Anders Graneheim, Swedish bodybuilder
- May 5 – Kaoru Wada, Japanese composer
- May 8 – Natalia Molchanova, Russian free-diver
- May 9
  - Dave Gahan, English singer-songwriter (Depeche Mode)
  - Paul Heaton, English singer-songwriter (The Housemartins, The Beautiful South)
- May 12 – Emilio Estevez, American actor
- May 13
  - Paul McDermott, Australian comedian
  - Eduardo Palomo, Mexican actor (d. 2003)
- May 14
  - Ian Astbury, English singer
  - Danny Huston, American actor and film director
- May 17
  - Lise Lyng Falkenberg, Danish writer
  - Craig Ferguson, Scottish actor and comedian
  - Kim Mulkey, American basketball player/coach
- May 18 – Sandra, German pop singer
- May 19 – Frances Ondiviela, Spanish/Mexican actress
- May 20 – Mike Jeffries, American soccer coach
- May 22 – Brian Pillman, American professional wrestler (d. 1997)
- May 24 – Gene Anthony Ray, American actor (d. 2003)
-

- May 26
  - Black, English singer-songwriter (d. 2016)
  - Genie Francis, American actress
  - Bobcat Goldthwait, American actor and comedian
- May 27 – Ravi Shastri, Indian cricketer
- May 28
  - Brandon Cruz, American child actor and punk rocker
  - François-Henri Pinault, French businessman
  - James Michael Tyler, American actor
- May 29 – Perry Fenwick, English actor
- May 30 – Timo Soini, Finnish politician
- May 31
  - Corey Hart, Canadian singer
  - Noriko Hidaka, Japanese voice actress
  - Sebastian Koch, German actor

June

Paula Abdul

Campino

Ollanta Humala

- June 1 – Sherri Howard, American athlete
- June 4
  - Paul Baloche, American Christian worship leader
  - John P. Kee, American gospel singer
- June 5 – Jeff Garlin, American comedian
- June 7 – Thierry Hazard, French singer and songwriter
- June 8 – Suzy Gorman, American photographer
- June 10
  - Gina Gershon, American actress and musician
  - Carolyn Hennesy, American actress
  - Ralf Schumann, German sport shooter
- June 11
  - Olga Charvátová, Czech alpine skier
  - Erika Salumäe, Estonian cyclist
  - Toshihiko Seki, Japanese voice actor
- June 12
  - Camilla Scott, Canadian actress
  - Jodi Thelen, American actress
- June 13
  - Ally Sheedy, American actress
  - Hannah Storm, American television personality
  - Bence Szabó, Hungarian fencer
- June 14 – Emilija Erčić, Yugoslav (Serbian) handball player
- June 15
  - Thomas Mikal Ford, American actor
  - Andrea Rost, Hungarian lyric soprano

- June 16 – Arnold Vosloo, South African actor
- June 17
  - Bap Kennedy, Northern Irish singer-songwriter
  - Lio, Belgian singer/actress
- June 18
  - Mitsuharu Misawa, Japanese professional wrestler (d. 2009)
  - Lisa Randall, American theoretical physicist
- June 19 – Paula Abdul, American dancer, choreographer and singer
- June 20 – Alex Di Gregorio, Italian editorial cartoonist
- June 21
  - Pipilotti Rist, Swiss video artist
  - Viktor Tsoi, Soviet underground singer and songwriter (d. 1990)
- June 22
  - Campino, German singer, band Die Toten Hosen
  - Stephen Chow, Hong Kong actor and director
  - Clyde Drexler, American basketball player
- June 23 – Kari Takko, Finnish ice hockey player
- June 26
  - Bussunda, Brazilian comedian (d. 2006)
  - Ollanta Humala, President of Peru
- June 27
  - Michael Ball, British stage actor and singer
  - Tony Leung Chiu-wai, Hong Kong actor
- June 28 – Don Chambers, American newspaper comic strip artist
- June 29
  - Amanda Donohoe, English actress
  - George Zamka, American astronaut
- June 30
  - Tony Fernández, Dominican baseball player
  - Deirdre Lovejoy, American actress
  - Julianne Regan, British singer/songwriter (All About Eve)

July

Tom Cruise

Wesley Snipes

- July 1 – Andre Braugher, American actor
- July 3
  - Tom Cruise, American actor
  - Thomas Gibson, American actor
- July 4
  - Neil Morrissey, British actor
  - Pam Shriver, American tennis player
- July 5 – Amrozi bin Nurhasyim, Indonesian terrorist (d. 2008)
- July 8 – Joan Osborne, American singer and songwriter
- July 11 – Pauline McLynn, Irish actress
- July 12
  - Dan Murphy, American rock guitarist (Soul Asylum)
  - Dean Wilkins, English football manager
- July 13
  - Tom Kenny, American voice actor and comedian
  - Zlata Petrović, Serbian pop singer

- July 14 – Jeff Olson, American percussionist (Trouble)
- July 15 – Michelle Ford, Australian swimmer
- July 16 – Grigory Leps, Russian singer
- July 18
  - Lee Arenberg, American actor
  - Jack Irons, American drummer
- July 19 – Anthony Edwards, American actor
- July 20
  - Carlos Alazraqui, American actor and comedian
  - Giovanna Amati, Italian race car driver
- July 21
  - Gabi Bauer, German journalist and television presenter
  - Rob Morrow, American actor
- July 23 – Eriq La Salle, American actor
- July 24 – Johnny O'Connell, American race car driver
- July 26
  - Galina Chistyakova, Ukrainian athlete
  - Sergey Kiriyenko, Prime Minister of Russia
- July 28 – Ray Shero, American hockey manager
- July 29 – Scott Steiner, American professional wrestler
- July 30
  - Alton Brown, American television host and chef
  - Lavinia Greenlaw, British poet and novelist
- July 31
  - Damien Frawley, Australian rugby union player
  - Wesley Snipes, American actor
  - John Laurinaitis, American professional wrestler

August

Steve Carell

Felipe Calderón Hinojosa

Dee Bradley Baker

- August 1 – Robert Clift, British field hockey player
- August 2 – Cynthia Stevenson, American actress
- August 4 – Roger Clemens, American baseball player
- August 5 – Patrick Ewing, Jamaican-born basketball player
- August 6 – Michelle Yeoh, Malaysian-born Hong Kong actress
-

- August 7
  - Doon Mackichan, British actress and comedian
  - Bruno Pelletier, Canadian singer
- August 8
  - Yūji Machi, Japanese voice actor
  - Mike Zanier, Canadian ice hockey player
- August 13 – John Slattery, American actor
- August 14 – Kevin Harris, Canadian skateboarder
- August 15 – Tom Colicchio, American chef
- August 16
  - Abdul-Majid al-Khoei, Twelver Shia cleric (d. 2003)
  - Christian Cameron, Canadian-American writer
  - Steve Carell, American actor and comedian
- August 17 – Pierre Sanoussi-Bliss, German actor and director
- August 18 – Felipe Calderón Hinojosa, President of Mexico
- August 19 – Valérie Kaprisky, French actress
- August 20
  - Sophie Aldred, British actress and television presenter
  - James Marsters, American actor
- August 21
  - Tsutomu Miyazaki, Japanese serial killer (d. 2008)
  - Gilberto Santa Rosa, Puerto Rican salsa singer
- August 23
  - Shaun Ryder, English musician, singer-songwriter, actor, television personality, author, and newspaper columnist
- August 24
  - Craig Kilborn, American talk show host
  - Mary Ellen Weber, American astronaut
- August 25 – Theresa Andrews, American swimmer
- August 26
  - Princess Lalla Meryem of Morocco
  - Bob Mionske, American cyclist and attorney
- August 27 – Vic Mignogna, American voice actor
- August 28 – David Fincher, American film director
- August 29
  - Ian James Corlett, Canadian voice actor

- o Jutta Kleinschmidt, German rally driver
- o Lycia Naff, American actress/journalist
- August 30 – Alexander Litvinenko, Russian ex-KGB colonel and ex-FSB lieutenant-colonel (d. 2006)
- August 31
  - o Dee Bradley Baker, American comedian, announcer and voice actor
  - o Mark L. Walberg, American television host and presenter

September

- September 1 – Ruud Gullit, Dutch footballer
- September 4 – Shinya Yamanaka, Japanese physician and researcher
- September 6 – Chris Christie, 55th governor of New Jersey
- September 7 – Kylie InGold, Australian fantasy artist
- September 8 – Thomas Kretschmann, German actor
- September 11
  - o Kristy McNichol, American actress
  - o Victoria Poleva, Ukrainian composer
  - o Andrew Jackson, Canadian voice actor
- September 12
  - o Dino Merlin, Bosnian singer-songwriter, musician and producer
  - o Amy Yasbeck, American actress
- September 13 – Hisao Egawa, Japanese voice actor
- September 15
  - o François Bloemhof, South African author
  - o Scott McNeil, Australian voice actor
- September 16 – Stephen Jones (Babybird), English singer and musician
- September 17 – Baz Luhrmann, Australian film director
- September 19 – Gottfried von Bismarck, German aristocrat and socialite (d. 2007)
- September 21 – Rob Morrow, American actor
- September 22 – Martin Crowe, New Zealand cricketer (d. 2016)

- September 24
  - Jack Dee, English comedian
  - Rosamund Kwan, Hong Kong actress
  - Ally McCoist, Scottish footballer and TV pundit
- September 25 – Aida Turturro, American actress
- September 26
  - Melissa Sue Anderson, American actress
  - Gregory Crewdson, American photographer
  - Steve Moneghetti, Australian long-distance runner
  - Al Pitrelli, American guitarist
  - Jacky Wu, Taiwanese talk show host, singer and actor
- September 27 – Kimberly Carson, American pornographic actress
- September 28 – Grant Fuhr, Canadian hockey player
- September 30 – Frank Rijkaard, Dutch football player and manager

October

Micky Flanagan

Michael Andretti

Joan Cusack

Evander Holyfield

David Furnish

- October 1
  - Micky Flanagan, English comedian
  - Esai Morales, American actor
- October 2 – James Hunter, English singer
- October 3 – Tommy Lee, American rock musician and drummer
- October 5
  - Michael Andretti, American race car driver
  - Caron Keating, British TV presenter (d. 2004)
- October 6 – Rich Yett, American baseball player
- October 11 – Joan Cusack, American actress and comedian
- October 12
  - Branko Crvenkovski, President of Macedonia

- Deborah Foreman, American actress
- October 13
  - T'Keyah Crystal Keymáh, American actress and comedian
  - Margareth Menezes, Brazilian singer
  - Kelly Preston, American actress
  - Jerry Rice, American football player
- October 16
  - Manute Bol, Sudanese basketball player and activist (d. 2010)
  - Flea, American rock bassist (Red Hot Chili Peppers)
  - Dmitri Hvorostovsky, Russian baritone
  - Durga McBroom, American singer (Blue Pearl)
  - Tamara McKinney, American alpine skier
- October 19
  - Tracy Chevalier, American author
  - Evander Holyfield, American boxer
- October 21 – Miki Itō, Japanese voice actress
- October 23
  - Doug Flutie, American football player
  - Mike Tomczak, American football player
- October 24 – Jay Novacek, American football player
- October 25
  - David Furnish, Canadian filmmaker, director and producer
  - Nick Hancock, British actor and television presenter
  - Darlene Vogel, American actress
- October 26 – Cary Elwes, British actor
- October 27
  - Jun'ichi Kanemaru, Japanese voice actor
  - Ang Peng Siong, Singaporean sportsman
- October 28 – Daphne Zuniga, American actress
- October 30 – Courtney Walsh, West Indian cricketer

November

Anthony Kiedis

Demi Moore

Jon Stewart

- November 1
  - Sharron Davies, British swimmer/television presenter
  - Magne Furuholmen, Norwegian musician (A-ha)
  - Anthony Kiedis, American rock singer (Red Hot Chili Peppers)
  -

- November 3
  - Gabe Newell, American business executive
  - Phil Katz, American computer programmer (d. 2000)
  - Jacqui Smith, UK politician
- November 6 – Aznil Nawawi, Malaysian TV host
- November 7 – Bettina Hoy, German equestrienne
- November 11
  - Gerard Horan, English actor
  - Mic Michaeli, Swedish keyboardist
  - Demi Moore, American actress
  - James Morrison, Australian musician
  - Nicole P. Stott, American astronaut
- November 12
  - Neal Shusterman, American author
  - Naomi Wolf, American feminist author and political consultant
- November 13 – Steve Altes, American humorist
- November 14
  - Jessica Straus, American voice actress
  - Atsuko Tanaka, Japanese voice actress
- November 15 – Judy Gold, American comedian and actress
- November 17 – Jamie Moyer, American baseball player
- November 18 – Kirk Hammett, American rock musician (Metallica)
- November 19
  - Jodie Foster, American actress and director
  - Sean Parnell, American politician
- November 21 – Steven Curtis Chapman, American Christian musician
- November 22 – Sumi Jo, Korean operatic soprano
- November 23 – Nicolás Maduro, president of Venezuela
- November 24 – John Kovalic, American cartoonist
- November 27 – Marumi Shiraishi, Japanese actress
- November 28 – Jon Stewart, American actor and comedian

- November 29
  - Andrew McCarthy, American actor
  - Ronny Jordan, English guitarist (d. 2014)
- November 30
  - Bo Jackson, American football and baseball player
  - Daniel Keys Moran, American writer

December

Felicity Huffman

- December 1
  - Sylvie Daigle, Canadian speed skater
  - Shōzō Hayashiya IX, Japanese rakugoka, tarento and voice actor
- December 3 – Tammy Jackson, American basketball player
- December 4
  - Julie Lemieux, Canadian voice actress
  - Anna Walker, British television presenter
- December 5 – José Cura, Argentine tenor
- December 6 – Janine Turner, American actress
- December 9
  - Albert Grajales, INTERPOL Director of Puerto Rico and martial artist
  - Felicity Huffman, American actress
- December 10 – Scott Capurro, American comedian
- December 11
  - Denise Biellmann, Swiss figure skater

- o Ben Browder, American actor
- December 12
  - o Tracy Austin, American tennis player
  - o Arturo Barrios, Mexican long-distance runner
  - o Max Raabe, German singer
- December 14 – Yvonne Ryding, Swedish pageant winner (Miss Universe 1984)
- December 16 – Maruschka Detmers, Dutch actress
- December 16 – Noel Garrett, Dean of Academic Support at Connecticut College
- December 17
  - o Paul Dobson, English footballer
  - o Richard Jewell, American security guard and media figure (d. 2007)
  - o Galina Malchugina, Russian athlete
  - o Rocco Mediate, American golfer
- December 19 – Jill Talley, American actress
- December 22 – Ralph Fiennes, English actor
- December 23 – Keiji Mutoh, Japanese professional wrestler
- December 27
  - o Mark Few, American basketball coach
  - o Bill Self, American basketball coach
  - o Sherri Steinhauer, American golfer
- December 28
  - o Michelle Cameron, Canadian synchronised swimmer
  - o Choi Soo-jong, South Korean actor
- December 30 – Alessandra Mussolini, Italian politician
- December 31 – Lance Reddick, American actor

Date unknown

- Gunnar Krantz, Swedish comic artist
- Nemat Shafik, Egyptian-born international banker.

Deaths

January

- January 4 – Hans Lammers, German Nazi minister (b. 1879)
- January 6 – Marziyya Davudova, Azerbaijani actress (b. 1901)
- January 13 – Ernie Kovacs, American TV comedian (b. 1919)
- January 16 – R. H. Tawney, English historian and social critic (b. 1880)
- January 19 – Snub Pollard, American actor (b. 1889)
- January 20 – Robinson Jeffers, American poet (b. 1887)
- January 26 – Lucky Luciano, American gangster (b. 1897)
- January 29 – Fritz Kreisler, Austrian violinist (b. 1875)

February

- February 1 – Carey Wilson, American screenwriter (b. 1889)
- February 2 – Shlomo Hestrin, Canadian-born Israeli biochemist (b. 1914)
- February 5 – Jacques Ibert, French composer (b. 1890)
- February 6
  - Roy Atwell, American actor, comedian and composer (b. 1878)
  - Cândido Portinari, Brazilian painter (b. 1903)
- February 7 – Clara Nordström, German writer and translator (b. 1886)
- February 10 – Eduard von Steiger, President of Switzerland (b. 1881)
- February 17
  - Joseph Kearns, American actor (b. 1907)
  - Bruno Walter, German conductor (b. 1876)
- February 19
  - James Barton, American actor (b. 1890)
  - Georgios Papanikolaou, Greek inventor (b. 1883)
- February 20 – Halliwell Hobbes, English-born film actor (b. 1877)
- February 24 – Hu Shih, Chinese liberal (b. 1891)
- February 27 – Willie Best, American actor (b. 1916)

- February 28 – Chic Johnson, American actor (b. 1891)

March

Arthur Compton

- March 1
  - Roscoe Ates, American actor (b. 1895)
  - Richard L. Conolly, American admiral (b. 1892)
  - W. Alton Jones, American industrialist and philanthropist (b. 1891)
  - Arnold Kirkeby, American hotelier, art collector and real estate investor (b. 1901)
  - Louise Lindner Eastman, American wife of Lee Eastman and mother of Linda McCartney (b. 1911)
  - Emelyn Whiton, American Olympic sailor (b. 1916)
- March 2 – Walt Kiesling, American football player (Chicago Cardinals) and a member of the Pro Football Hall of Fame (b. 1903)
- March 15 – Arthur Compton, American physicist, Nobel Prize laureate (b. 1892)
- March 20 – C. Wright Mills, American sociologist (b. 1916)
- March 24
  - Jean Goldkette, Greek-born jazz musician (b. 1899)
  - Auguste Piccard, Swiss physicist and explorer (b. 1884)

April

- April 1 – Jussi Kekkonen, Finnish major (b. 1910)

- April 3 – Benny Paret, Cuban welterweight boxer (died as result of injuries in the ring; b. 1937)
- April 10
  - Michael Curtiz, Austrian-born film director (b. 1886)
  - Manton S. Eddy, U.S. general (b. 1892)
  - Stuart Sutcliffe, British artist and pop guitarist (The Beatles; b. 1940)
- April 13 – Culbert Olson, Governor of California (b. 1876)
- April 15
  - Clara Blandick, American actress (b. 1880)
  - Arsenio Lacson, Filipino politician and sportswriter (b. 1911)
- April 17 – Louise Fazenda, American actress (b. 1895)
- April 21 – Sir Frederick Handley Page, English aircraft manufacturer (b. 1885)
- April 22 – Vera Reynolds, American actress (b. 1899)
- April 24 – Milt Franklyn, American film composer (b. 1897)

May

- May 5 – Ernest Tyldesley, English cricketer (b. 1889)
- May 13
  - Henry Trendley Dean, American dental researcher (b. 1893)
  - Franz Kline, American painter (b. 1910)
- May 27 – Egon Petri, German pianist (b. 1881)
- May 28 – Robert Francis Anthony Studds, American admiral and engineer, fourth Director of the United States Coast and Geodetic Survey (b. 1896)
- May 31
  - Henry Fountain Ashurst, American politician (b. 1874)
  - Adolf Eichmann, Nazi war criminal (b. 1906)

June

- June 1 – Adolf Eichmann, German SS officer and a major organiser of the Holocaust (executed) (b. 1906)
- June 2 – Vita Sackville-West, English writer and landscape gardener (b. 1892)

- June 4 – Charles William Beebe, American oceanic pioneer (b. 1877)
- June 6
  - Yves Klein, French painter (b. 1928)
  - Guinn Williams, American actor (b. 1899)
- June 7 – Korneli Kekelidze, Georgian philologist (b. 1879)
- June 8 – Eugène Freyssinet, French civil engineer (b. 1879)
- June 12 – John Ireland, English composer (b. 1879)
- June 13 – Sir Eugene Goossens, English composer (b. 1893)
- June 15 – Alfred Cortot, Swiss pianist (b. 1877)
- June 19
  - Frank Borzage, American film director (b. 1894)
  - Will Wright, American character actor (b. 1891)
- June 24 – Lucile Watson, Canadian actress (b. 1879)
- June 27 – Paul Viiding, Estonian poet, author and literary critic (b. 1904)
- June 28 – Mickey Cochrane, American baseball player (Philadelphia Athletics) and a member of the MLB Hall of Fame (b. 1903)

July

William Faulkner

- July 1 – Bidhan Chandra Roy, Indian physician and politician, Chief Minister of West Bengal (b. 1882)
- July 4 – Rex Bell, American actor (b. 1903)
- July 6
  - Paul Boffa, Maltese politician, 5th Prime Minister of Malta (1947–1950) (b. 1890)

- ○ William Faulkner, American writer, Nobel Prize laureate (b. 1897)
- ○ Archduke Joseph August of Austria, Austrian field marshal (b. 1872)
- July 8 – Georges Bataille, French writer (b. 1897)
- July 10 – Yehuda Leib Maimon, Bassarabian-born Israeli rabbi and government minister (b. 1875)
- July 12 – Roger Wolfe Kahn, American band leader (b. 1907)
- July 13 – Jerry Wald, American screenwriter and producer (b. 1911)
- July 21 – G. M. Trevelyan, English historian (b. 1876)
- July 23 – Victor Moore, American actor (b. 1876)
- July 29 – Leonardo De Lorenzo, Italian flautist (b. 1875)
- July 27 – Richard Aldington, English poet (b. 1892)
- July 30 – Myron McCormick, American actor (b. 1908)

August

Marilyn Monroe

- August 5 – Marilyn Monroe, American actress (b. 1926)
- August 6 – Ángel Borlenghi, Argentine labor leader and politician (b. 1904)
- August 9 – Hermann Hesse, German-born writer, Nobel Prize laureate (b. 1877)
- August 15 – Lei Feng, Chinese soldier (b. 1940)
- August 18 – Cleo Ridgely, American actress (b. 1893)
- August 23 – Hoot Gibson, American actor (b. 1892)
- August 24 – Mykolas Biržiška, Lithuanian politician (b. 1882)

- August 27 – Leopoldo Panero, Spanish poet (b. 1909)
- August 28 – John Collum, American actor (b. 1926)

September

戏 陽 予 倩

Ouyang Yuqian

- September 1 – Hans-Jürgen von Arnim, German general (b. 1889)
- September 3 – E. E. Cummings, American poet (b. 1894)
- September 6 – Hanns Eisler, German-born composer (b. 1898)
- September 7
  - Karen Blixen, Danish writer (b. 1885)
  - Morris Louis, American painter (b. 1912)
  - Graham Walker, English motorcycle racer (b. 1896)
- September 18 – Ahmad bin Yahya, King of Yemen (b. 1891)
- September 19 – Nikolai Pogodin, Soviet playwright (b. 1900)
- September 20 – Conrad Helfrich, Dutch admiral (b. 1886)
- September 21 – Ouyang Yuqian, Chinese playwright, director and Peking opera performer (b. 1889)
- September 23
  - Louis de Soissons, Canadian-born English architect (b. 1890)
  - Patrick Hamilton, English dramatist (b. 1904)
- September 24
  - Sam McDaniel, American actor (b. 1886)
  - Charles Reisner, American silent film actor and director (b. 1887)
- September 30 – Bernard Rawlings, British admiral (b. 1889)

October

Eleanor Roosevelt

- October 2
    - Henry Louis Larsen, American Marine Corps general; Governor of American Samoa and Governor of Guam (b. 1890)
    - Frank Lovejoy, American actor (b. 1912)
- October 6 – Tod Browning, American film director (b. 1882)
- October 9 – Milan Vidmar, Slovenian chess player (b. 1885)
- October 10 – Stancho Belkovski, Bulgarian architect and lecturer (b. 1891)
- October 20 – Jesús Herrera, Spanish international footballer (b. 1938)
- October 26 – Louise Beavers, American actress (b. 1902)
- October 27 – Enrico Mattei, Italian politician (plane crash) (b. 1906)

November

Niels Bohr

Wilhelmina of the Netherlands

- November 7 – Eleanor Roosevelt, First Lady of the United States (b. 1884)
- November 15 – Irene Lentz, American costume designer (b. 1900)
- November 18 – Niels Bohr, Danish physicist, Nobel Prize laureate (b. 1885)
- November 22 – René Coty, 17th President of France (b. 1882)
- November 28
  - K. C. Dey, Indian singer, composer, actor and teacher (b. 1893)
  - Queen Wilhelmina of the Netherlands (b. 1880)
- November 29 – Erik Scavenius, former Prime Minister of Denmark (b. 1877)
- November 30 – Joseph Lade Pawsey, Australian radio astronomer. (b. 1908)

December

- December 6 – Harry Bauler, American politician (b. 1910)
- December 7 – Kirsten Flagstad, Norwegian soprano (b. 1895)
- December 10 – Robert C. Giffen, American admiral (b. 1886)
- December 13 – John Cunningham, British admiral (b. 1885)
- December 15 – Charles Laughton, English actor and director (b. 1899)
- December 16 – Lew Landers, American TV and film director (b. 1901)
- December 17 – Thomas Mitchell, American actor (b. 1892)
- December 18 – Garrett Mattingly, American historian (b. 1900)

- December 20 – Emil Artin, Austrian mathematician (b. 1898)
- December 24 – Wilhelm Ackermann, German mathematician (b. 1896)

Unknown

- Henry Matthew Talintyre, British comic strip artist (b. 1893)

Nobel Prizes

- Physics – Lev Landau
- Chemistry – Max Perutz, John Kendrew
- Physiology or Medicine – Francis Crick, James Watson, Maurice Wilkins
- Literature – John Steinbeck
- Peace – Linus Pauling

In the News

Heavy storm flood on Germany's North Sea coast, mainly around Hamburg, more than 300 people die, thousands losing their homes.

Cuban Missile Crisis when USSR plans to deploy Missiles in Cuba brings the world to the brink of world war.

Marilyn Monroe is found dead on August 5th after apparently overdosing on sleeping pills.

The US Navy SEALS are created on January 1st as the U.S. Navy's principal special operations force.

The First Wal-Mart discount store is opened by by Sam Walton in Bentonville Arkansas.

The Space Needle an observation tower in Seattle, Washington is completed in time for the 1962 World's Fair.

Brazil beat Czechoslovakia 3-1 to win the 1962 World Cup.

First Ever Flavored Crisps / Chips sold Salt and Vinegar.

John H. Glenn, Jr., becomes first American to orbit the earth during Friendship 7 orbit.

Popular Films - West Side Story, Spartacus, El Cid.

1962 Calendar

January 1962
Sun	Mon	Tue	Wed	Thu	Fri	Sat
	1	2	3	4	5	6
7	8	9	10	11	12	13
14	15	16	17	18	19	20
21	22	23	24	25	26	27
28	29	30	31			

February 1962
Sun	Mon	Tue	Wed	Thu	Fri	Sat
				1	2	3
4	5	6	7	8	9	10
11	12	13	14	15	16	17
18	19	20	21	22	23	24
25	26	27	28			

March 1962
Sun	Mon	Tue	Wed	Thu	Fri	Sat
				1	2	3
4	5	6	7	8	9	10
11	12	13	14	15	16	17
18	19	20	21	22	23	24
25	26	27	28	29	30	31

April 1962
Sun	Mon	Tue	Wed	Thu	Fri	Sat
1	2	3	4	5	6	7
8	9	10	11	12	13	14
15	16	17	18	19	20	21
22	23	24	25	26	27	28
29	30					

May 1962
Sun	Mon	Tue	Wed	Thu	Fri	Sat
		1	2	3	4	5
6	7	8	9	10	11	12
13	14	15	16	17	18	19
20	21	22	23	24	25	26
27	28	29	30	31		

June 1962
Sun	Mon	Tue	Wed	Thu	Fri	Sat
					1	2
3	4	5	6	7	8	9
10	11	12	13	14	15	16
17	18	19	20	21	22	23
24	25	26	27	28	29	30

July 1962
Sun	Mon	Tue	Wed	Thu	Fri	Sat
1	2	3	4	5	6	7
8	9	10	11	12	13	14
15	16	17	18	19	20	21
22	23	24	25	26	27	28
29	30	31				

August 1962
Sun	Mon	Tue	Wed	Thu	Fri	Sat
			1	2	3	4
5	6	7	8	9	10	11
12	13	14	15	16	17	18
19	20	21	22	23	24	25
26	27	28	29	30	31	

September 1962
Sun	Mon	Tue	Wed	Thu	Fri	Sat
						1
2	3	4	5	6	7	8
9	10	11	12	13	14	15
16	17	18	19	20	21	22
23	24	25	26	27	28	29
30						

October 1962
Sun	Mon	Tue	Wed	Thu	Fri	Sat
	1	2	3	4	5	6
7	8	9	10	11	12	13
14	15	16	17	18	19	20
21	22	23	24	25	26	27
28	29	30	31			

November 1962
Sun	Mon	Tue	Wed	Thu	Fri	Sat
				1	2	3
4	5	6	7	8	9	10
11	12	13	14	15	16	17
18	19	20	21	22	23	24
25	26	27	28	29	30	

December 1962
Sun	Mon	Tue	Wed	Thu	Fri	Sat
						1
2	3	4	5	6	7	8
9	10	11	12	13	14	15
16	17	18	19	20	21	22
23	24	25	26	27	28	29
30	31					

www.ingramcontent.com/pod-product-compliance
Lightning Source LLC
Chambersburg PA
CBHW060648290526
45793CB00001B/445